MILITARY MISSIONS

COUNTERTERRORISM

BY NEL YOMTOV

BELLWETHER MEDIA • MINNEAPOLIS, MN

EPIC

EPIC BOOKS are no ordinary books. They burst with intense action, high-speed heroics, and shadows of the unknown. Are you ready for an Epic adventure?

This edition first published in 2017 by Bellwether Media, Inc.

No part of this publication may be reproduced in whole or in part without written permission of the publisher.
For information regarding permission, write to Bellwether Media, Inc., Attention: Permissions Department, 5357 Penn Avenue South, Minneapolis, MN 55419.

Library of Congress Cataloging-in-Publication Data

Names: Yomtov, Nelson, author.
Title: Counterterrorism / by Nel Yomtov.
Description: Minneapolis, MN : Bellwether Media, Inc., 2017. | Series: Epic:
  Military Missions | Audience: Grades 2 through 7. | Includes bibliographical references and index.
Identifiers: LCCN 2015051498 | ISBN 9781626174344 (hardcover : alk. paper)
Subjects: LCSH: Terrorism–Juvenile literature. | Terrorism–Prevention–Juvenile literature.
Classification: LCC HV6431 .Y66 2017 | DDC 363.325/17–dc23
LC record available at http://lccn.loc.gov/2015051498

Printed in the United States of America, North Mankato, MN.

TABLE OF CONTENTS

GUNFIRE AT NIGHT

United States Army **Delta Force** operators sneak through the night. They are on a mission to get enemy weapons.

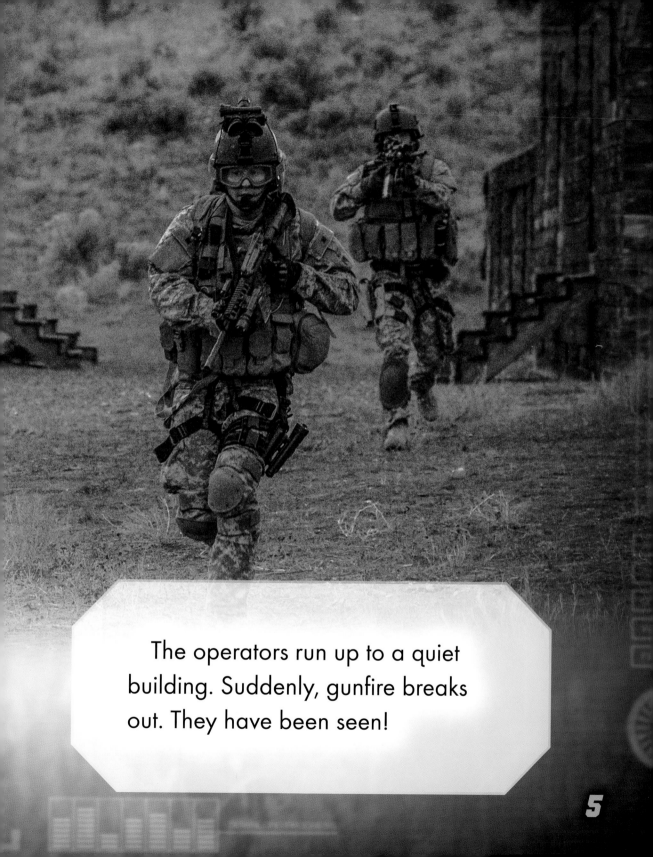

The operators run up to a quiet building. Suddenly, gunfire breaks out. They have been seen!

The operators fire back. They run into the building. The enemy quickly escapes.

But the Delta Force team collects the supply of weapons. The operators have saved many **innocent** lives!

THE MISSION

Counterterrorism missions keep the enemy from hurting people. They are often done in secret.

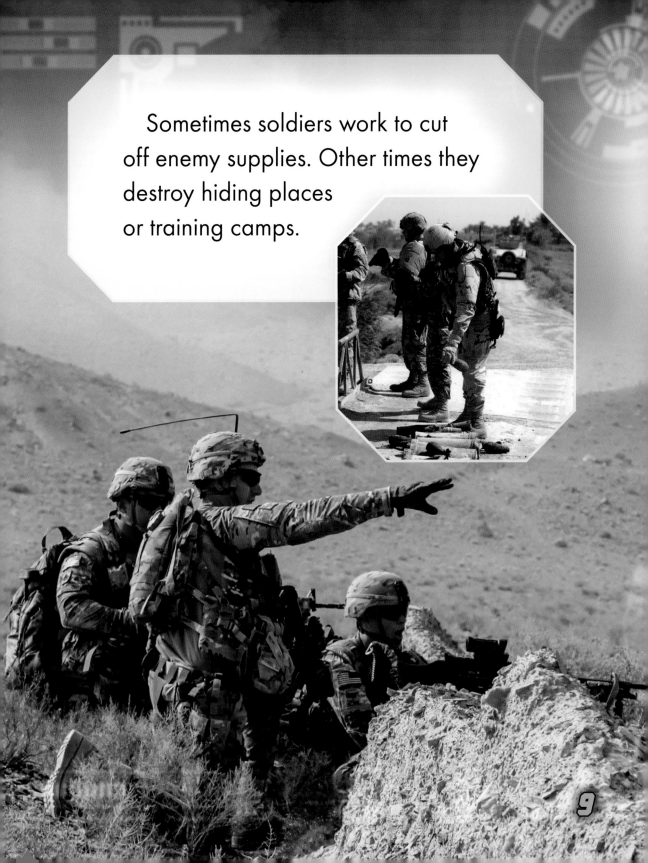

Sometimes soldiers work to cut off enemy supplies. Other times they destroy hiding places or training camps.

Many missions focus on finding people. Soldiers go after **terrorist** leaders. Sometimes they rescue **hostages**.

They also gather **intelligence**. They work with other countries to fight terrorism.

hostage rescue

A DAMAGING BLOW

Many missions keep terrorist groups from gaining new members.

REAL-LIFE COUNTERTERRORISM

What: Operation Desert Storm

Who: U.S. Army Delta Force

Where: Western Iraq

When: 1991

Why: Knock out Scud missiles aimed at Israel

How: Delta Force operators destroyed the missiles during nightly missions

Operators inspect a destroyed Scud missile

terrorist capture

THE PLAN

Missions can be close **combat** or long-range shooting. Troops carry **carbines** and pistols. Some use **sniper rifles**.

sniper rifle

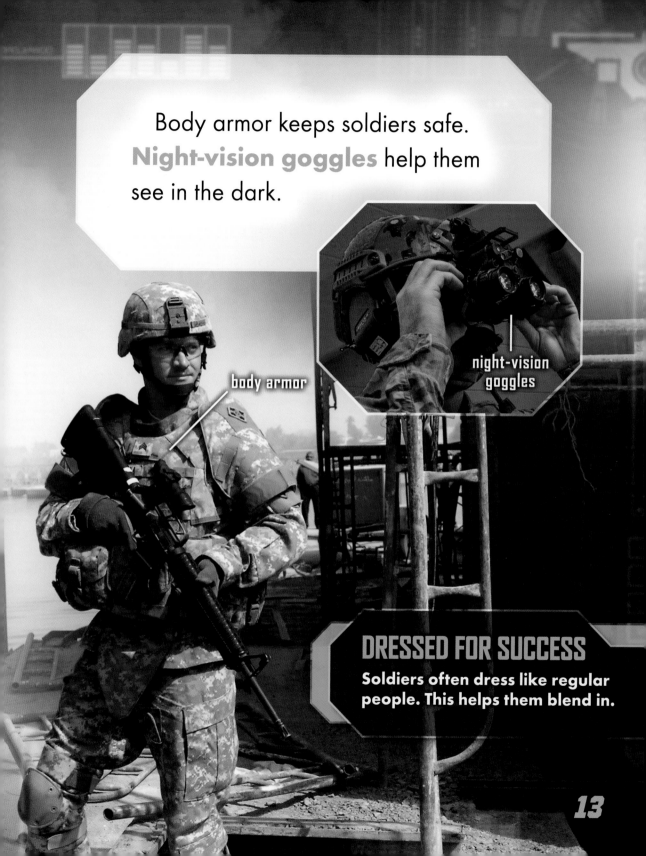

Body armor keeps soldiers safe. **Night-vision goggles** help them see in the dark.

body armor

night-vision goggles

DRESSED FOR SUCCESS

Soldiers often dress like regular people. This helps them blend in.

Other counterterrorism missions use **drones**. These aircraft spy from high up in the air.

Some drones attack enemy targets. They keep troops safe and ready for other missions.

MQ-9 Reaper drone

COUNTERTERRORISM EQUIPMENT AND GEAR

HK416 carbine

Glock 19 pistol

Barrett M107 sniper rifle

night-vision goggles

Raven drone

THE TEAM

All U.S. military branches have groups that fight terrorism. Delta Force was created for this purpose.

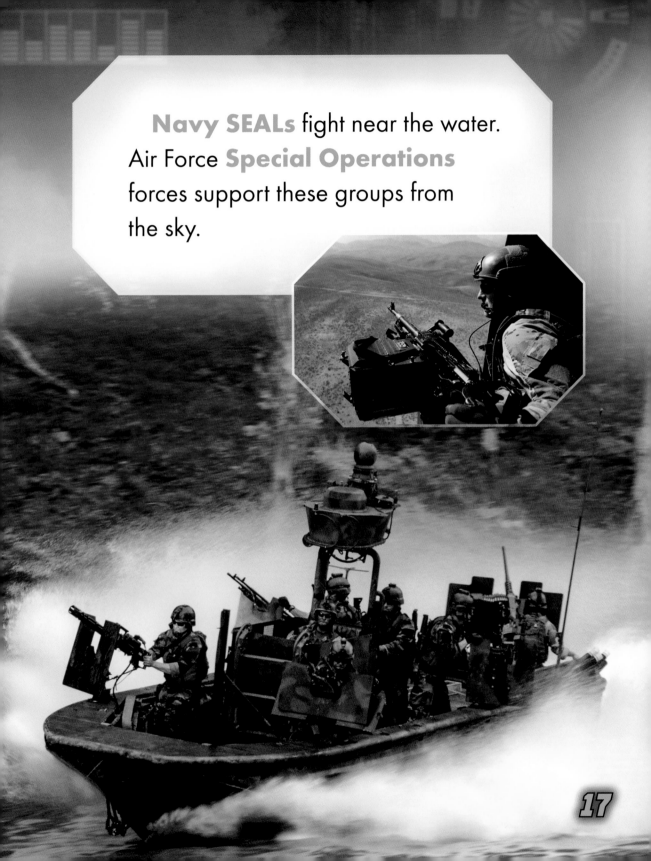

Navy **SEALs** fight near the water. Air Force **Special Operations** forces support these groups from the sky.

Members of counterterrorism groups have many years of training. They learn general and special combat skills.

SPEAK UP

Delta Force operators learn to speak other languages. This helps them work in faraway places.

They also learn how to teach others. They help other countries fight terrorism.

ACCOMPLISHED!

Counterterrorism missions take many forms. But they all work to keep people safe.

Every day, the U.S. military protects innocent people around the world!

PAYING THE COST

The U.S. spends more than $16 billion on counterterrorism each year.

GLOSSARY

carbines—small, lightweight guns

combat—fighting between soldiers or armies

Delta Force—a small force within the United States Army that fights terrorism

drones—unmanned military aircraft controlled by remotes

hostages—people who are captured by a person or group that wants something in exchange for their freedom

innocent—not deserving to be harmed

intelligence—information about an enemy's position, movements, or weapons

Navy SEALs—a small force of the United States Navy that carries out special operations; Navy SEALs are trained to fight on sea, air, and land.

night-vision goggles—special eyewear that allows the user to see in the dark

sniper rifles—guns designed to be shot from hiding places

Special Operations—military missions carried out by specially trained forces that use uncommon practices

terrorist—a person who uses violence to try to get something

TO LEARN MORE

AT THE LIBRARY

Gordon, Nick. *Army Delta Force*. Minneapolis, Minn.: Bellwether Media, 2013.

Lusted, Marcia Amidon. *Army Delta Force: Elite Operations*. Minneapolis, Minn.: Lerner Publications, 2014.

Markovics, Joyce. *Today's Army Heroes*. New York, N.Y.: Bearport Publishing, 2012.

ON THE WEB

Learning more about counterterrorism is as easy as 1, 2, 3.

1. Go to www.factsurfer.com.

2. Enter "counterterrorism" into the search box.

3. Click the "Surf" button and you will see a list of related web sites.

With factsurfer.com, finding more information is just a click away.

INDEX

The images in this book are reproduced through the courtesy of: Przemek Tokar, front cover (left); United States Department of Defense/ DVIDS, front cover (top right), pp. 4, 5, 6, 7, 9, 9 (top), 10, 11, 12, 13, 15 (bottom right), 17, 17 (top), 18, 19; Oleg Zabielin, front cover (bottom right); bibiphoto, p. 8; United States Department of Defense/ Wikipedia, 11 (top); U.S. Air Force Photo/ Alamy, p. 14; Dybdal/ Wikipedia, 15 (top left); NSC Photography, p. 15 (top right); Heavennearth/ Wikipedia, p. 15 (middle); alessandro guerriero, p. 15 (bottom left); Philipp Guelland/ Getty Images, p. 16; 615 collection/ Alamy, p. 20; U.S. Navy Photo/ Alamy, p. 21.